623.8
Bu
copy1

BOATS

FIRST LOOK AT

Library of Congress Cataloging-in-Publication Data

Butler, Daphne, 1945-
    [Boats]
    First look at boats / Daphne Butler.
        p. cm. – (First look)
    Previously published as: Boats. c1990.
    Includes bibliographical references and index.
    Summary: A simple introduction to different kinds of boats and
their uses.
    ISBN 0-8368-0502-X
    1. Boats–Juvenile literature. [1. Boats.] I. Title. II. Series: Butler,
Daphne, 1945- First look.
VM150.B87 1991
623.82–dc20
                                                                90-10256

North American edition first published in 1991 by

Gareth Stevens Children's Books
1555 North RiverCenter Drive, Suite 201
Milwaukee, Wisconsin 53212, USA

U.S. edition copyright © 1991 by Gareth Stevens, Inc. First published as *Boats* in Great
Britain, copyright © 1990, by Simon & Schuster Young Books. Additional end matter
copyright © 1991 by Gareth Stevens, Inc.

Photographs: ZEFA

Series editor: Rita Reitci
Design: M&M Design Partnership
Cover design: Laurie Shock

Printed in the United States of America

1 2 3 4 5 6 7 8 9 9 7 96 95 94 93 92 91

BOATS

FIRST LOOK AT

DAPHNE BUTLER

Gareth Stevens Children's Books
MILWAUKEE

Books in the
FIRST LOOK series:

CONTENTS

OVER THE ROCKS

The river is rushing down the mountain over the rocks. Canoes and rafts float on the water. Paddlers steer them past the rocks.

Look at these boats. Why do you think they float?

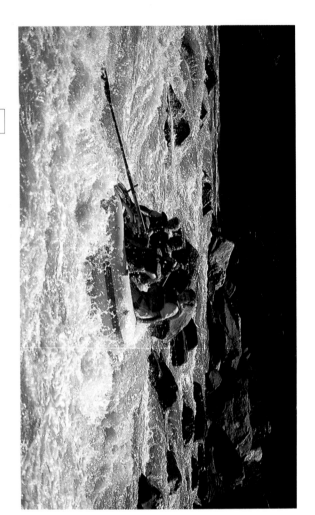

7

WIDE AND SLOW

The wide river flows slowly across the flat land.
The water is calmer here than in the mountains.
This is a good place for rowing or learning to sail.

What makes these boats move through the water?

BOATS WITH ENGINES

Barges carry loads of goods on the river. The load is called cargo. Other boats carry passengers.

These boats are big and heavy and have engines to push them through the water.

AT THE SEA

The river has reached the sea. Fishing boats are tied up along the banks of the river.

The boats sail out to sea to catch fish. They drag their nets behind them in the water.

13

TAKE A FERRY

Ferryboats carry people, cars, trucks, buses, and even railroad cars! The cars, buses, and trucks are carefully loaded onto the ferry.

This is a heavy boat. Why do you think it floats?

AT THE PORT

Huge boats are loaded with cargo packed into boxes called containers.

Can you see the containers on the deck? The boat must be very heavy.

Does all cargo travel in containers?

HOW MUCH CARGO?

This boat is empty, so it is floating high in the water. When it is loaded with cargo, it sinks down.

Can you see the numbers on the back of the boat? The water comes up to a number when the boat is loaded. The number tells how much cargo is in the boat.

TUGBOATS

Some cargo boats are so huge that they cannot move easily inside the port.

They need small boats called tugboats to tow them in and out.

21

PASSENGER BOATS

People sail around the world in big boats called cruise ships. A ship like this would take five weeks to sail from New York to Australia.

Is there a faster way to get to and from Australia?

ON THE BRIDGE

This man is the captain of the ship. He steers the ship from a room called the bridge. He has many instruments to help him.

A large boat takes a long time to slow down or turn. Why do you think this is so?

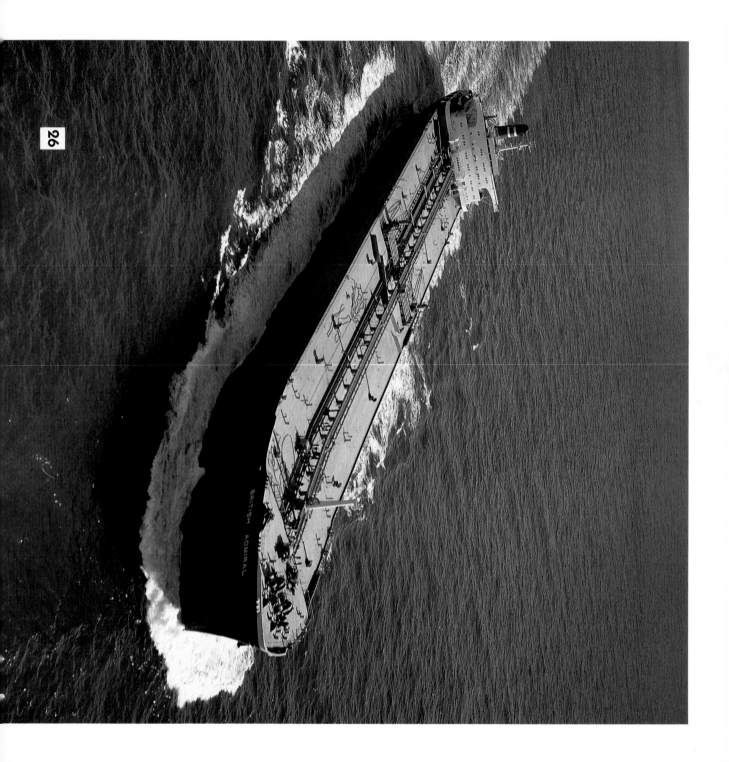

OUT TO SEA

The captain must look out for dangers at sea. Because big boats turn slowly, the captain must keep a safe distance from rocks and other boats.

Can you think of other dangers?

BEFORE ENGINES

Large boats have engines to push them through the water. The bigger the boat, the more powerful the engine must be.

How did boats move through the water before engines were invented?

More Books about Boats

Boat Book. Gibbons (Holiday)

Boating with Cap'n Bob and Matey: An Encyclopedia for Kids of All Ages. (Seascape Enterprises)

Canoeing is for Me. Moran (Lerner)

Cargo Ships and the People Who Work Them. Ancona (Harper & Row Junior Books)

Finding Out about Things that Float. Thomas (EDC)

Let's Discover Ships and Boats. (Raintree)

Mississippi Sternwheelers. Zeck (Carolrhoda)

The Raft. Haskell (Kennebec River)

Sailing. Barrett (Franklin Watts)

Ships. Barrett (Franklin Watts)

Ships and Seaports. Carter (Childrens Press)

Ships and the River. Canright (South Street Seaport Museum)

Glossary

Barge: A wide boat with a flat bottom that carries heavy cargo up and down rivers and canals. Some barges have engines. Others are towed by tugboats.

Bridge: A room set high over the deck that contains the boat's controls. The captain sails the boat from inside the bridge.

Canoe: A narrow, light boat with pointed ends. Sometimes it has a cover over it to keep out the water. Paddles are used to move a canoe.

Cargo: The load of goods carried by a boat, airplane, train, or truck. Cargo is also called freight.

Cargo boat: Smaller than a passenger cruise ship, a boat that carries cargo in rooms called holds. Some cargo boats are specially made to carry containers, bulk cargoes like wheat or gravel, or liquids such as oil.

Containers: Big metal boxes of the same size used for moving cargo. It is easier to load and unload a boat when the cargo is in containers. People can move the containers quickly from a boat onto a train or a truck.

Cruise ship: A very big boat that carries passengers on long trips over the sea. The passengers eat, sleep, and play on the cruise ship.

Deck: A platform that is used as a floor on a boat. Boats can have several decks, one over the other.

Ferryboat: A boat used to take cars, trucks, buses, and people on short trips across water. Some ferryboats carry railroad cars.

Fishing boat: A boat used for catching fish to sell. Fishing boats drag nets behind to gather the fish.

Port: A city or a town on the sea or a lake with a place where boats can load and unload cargo.

Raft: A flat structure, like a platform, that floats on water. A raft can be made of rubber, or of logs, planks, or barrels fastened together.

Tugboat: A strongly built, powerful boat made for towing or pushing much bigger boats in small spaces, like a port or a canal. Tugboats also tow barges up and down rivers.

Index

A number that is in **boldface** type means that the page has a picture of the subject on it.